Animal Wo...

THE TIGER

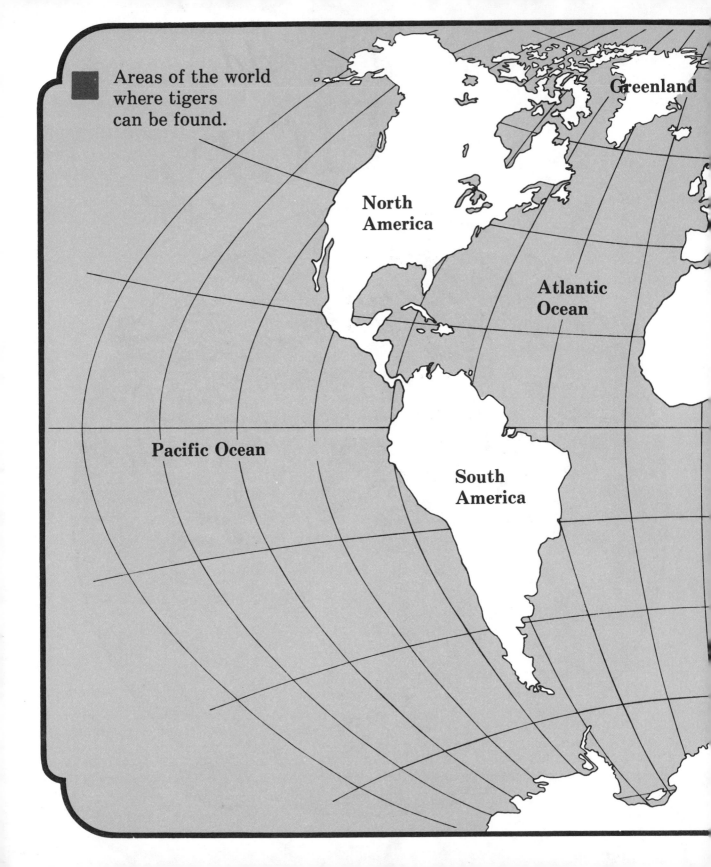

Areas of the world where tigers can be found.

North America

Greenland

Atlantic Ocean

Pacific Ocean

South America

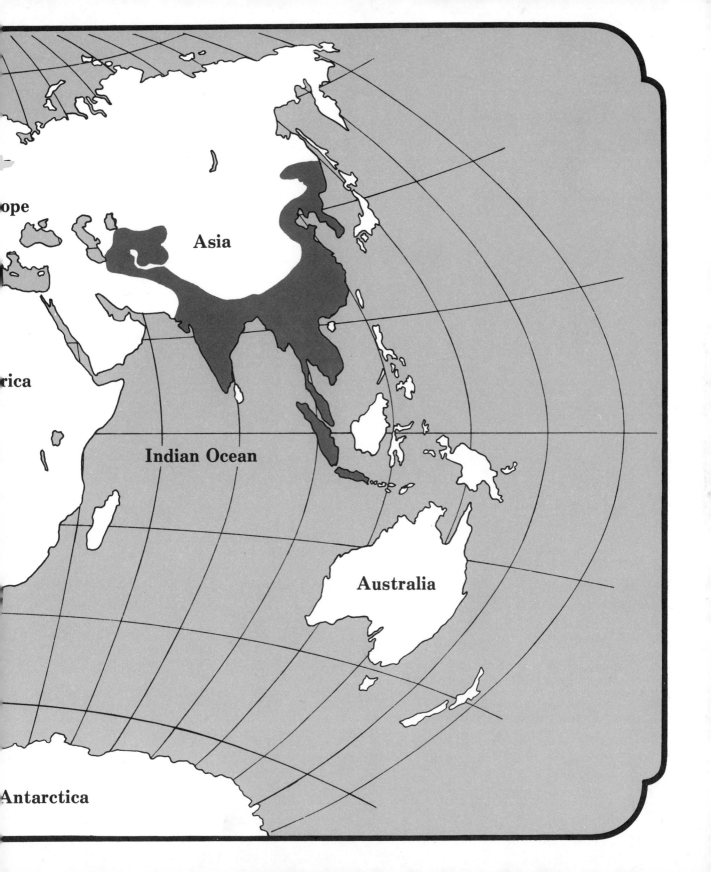

Published by Watermill Press, an imprint of Troll Associates, Inc.
Copyright © 1983 by The Rourke Enterprises, Inc. All copyrights reserved. No part of this book may be reproduced in any form without written permission from the publisher. Printed in the United States of America.

10 9 8 7 6 5 4 3 2

Library of Congress Cataloging in Publication Data

Saunier, Nadine.
  The tiger.

  (Animal world)
  Translation of: Le tigre.
  Reprint. Originally published: London : Macdonald
Educational, 1981.
  Summary: Text and illustrations introduce the physical
characteristics, habits, and natural environment of the
tiger.
  1. Tigers—Juvenile literature.   [1. Tigers]
I. Graham, Tony, ill.   II. Title.   III. Series.
QL737.C23S2813   1984   599.74'428   83-9785
ISBN 0-86592-866-5

Animal World
THE TIGER

illustrated by
Tony Graham

Watermill Press

The tiger's home

The sun beats down on the lowlands at the foot of the
towering peaks of the Himalayas. A yellow shape moves
silently through the tall grass. It is the mother
tiger returning from a hunt to her lair. Three little
cubs wait eagerly for her. As soon as she gets back
she will feed them. They are only two weeks old, but
their eyes are open and bright. They will drink only
their mother's milk for another six weeks. Then they
will leave the safety of their hidden home.

Early days

The tiger cubs go outside for the first time. Everything seems new and fresh to them as they chase playfully after a leaf, or pretend to wrestle with each other. They pat each other with their big, floppy paws.

They are only pretending to bite and claw and are not really hurting each other. It is useful practice for the days when they will have to look after themselves. The tigress is never far away.

Keeping safe

Each tiger lives on its own patch of land, called a
territory. The tigress marks out the edge of her
territory every few days by spraying the bushes with
urine. Any other tigers will stay away.

A male is near

A loud roar rumbles across the plain. The tigress recognizes the sound of a male and stops dead. She gathers the cubs close to her where they are safe. The male is a lone hunter, strong and powerful. He weighs about 450 pounds and can be up to 9½ feet long. Even so, he can run very fast over short distances. His hunting territory is many square miles.

Hunting

The tigers prick up their ears and listen carefully.
Their stripes hide them as they walk through the long
grass. It is a perfect camouflage. The nearby buffalo
cannot see them.

The cubs are now eight months old and big enough
to hunt for themselves. For the last time the tigress
comes to help the cubs make the kill. There is a
short, speedy sprint and a pounce.

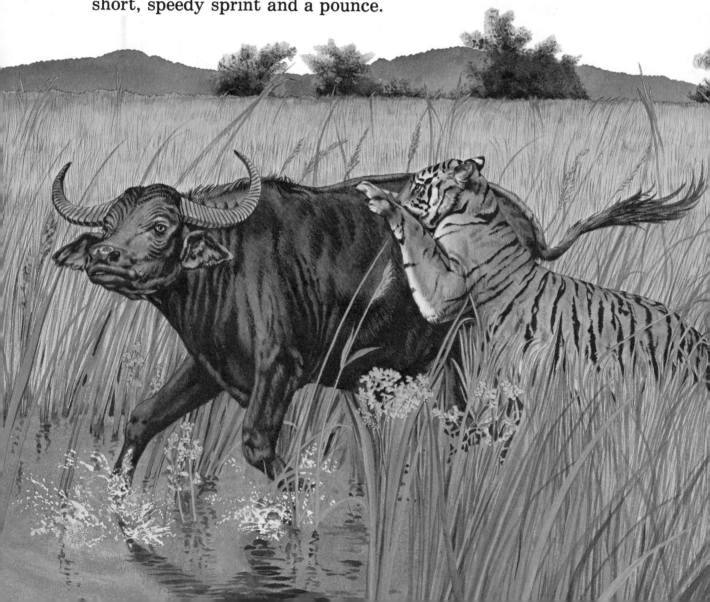

The tigress leaps onto the buffalo's neck and breaks its back. She will drag the body somewhere safe and the whole family will eat it for a few days. When all the meat has been eaten, the bones will be hidden.

The tigress will now stay with her cubs, but they will hunt on their own. They will eat deer and wild pigs, or smaller animals like monkeys. Sometimes they will eat fish or insects.

A human is near

Suddenly the forest animals sense that a person is
near. The monkeys chatter and scamper away, and a
parrot flaps off to safety. The tigers also smell the
man and slink away. Many people hunt tigers for
their skin. Because of people's greed, six of the eight
species of tiger are in danger of extinction.

Water games

Splash! The tiger leaps into the cool water and swims away. Unlike most members of the cat family, tigers love water and are strong swimmers. The young follow their mother who is searching for fish and frogs. They play games, splashing and paddling in the shallows.

Other animals who have come to have a drink at the
river go away quietly. They do not want to be
spotted by the frightening tigers, and become their
next meal! The tigers do not notice and continue
playing.

Tigers have lived in many countries all over Asia.
Some people think that they might have travelled from
one place to another across the sea by swimming.

Parting

When the baby tigers are two years old, their mother leaves them. They are old enough to live alone. They have reddish-brown fur with creamy-white bellies and a ruff of long fur around their necks. Blackish-brown lines zigzag across their sleek bodies.

They have learned all the rules of the jungle. Their sight is perfect, and their hearing sharp. They can trap their prey. The mother stalks off into the long grass, leaving the youngsters to find and protect their own territories.

Mating time

The tigress is now ready to find a mate. She moans and a piercing shriek comes through the jungle in return. A male is near. The two tigers make friends. They stay together for a while and mate. Then they will separate again. In about three months' time a new litter of blind, mewing cubs will be born.

SOME INTERESTING FACTS ABOUT TIGERS

Species:

Tigers are mammals, which belong to the cat family. All tigers live in Asia. It appears that they originated in northern Asia. They migrated from eastern Siberia southwards to China and India. A westward migration took them from Mongolia to the Caucasus.

Tigers vary in size and appearance. They are the largest members of the cat family. The scientific name for the tiger is Felidea Carnivora. "Felidea" tells us the animal is in the cat family. "Carnivora" means that it is a meat eater. In fact, cats are the most purely carnivorous of all carnivores. The cat family includes tigers, lions, jaguars, leopards, cheetahs, pumas, lynxes, ocelots, right down to the common domestic cat.

A famous ancestor of the tiger is the saber-toothed tiger. It lived about 40 million years ago. It got its name from the two curved tusks coming out of its mouth.

Description:

Although they are all basically the same, tigers differ in coloration and body build. The tiger's appearance has a lot to do with where it lives. Tigers in cold climates tend to have pale, thick, long fur. Tigers living in warm climates have shorter, orange-colored fur.

A tiger's body is built for speed and flexibility. They are large and muscular animals, but very quick and light on their feet. They rarely climb. Unlike most cats, they like to bathe and they are good swimmers.

Cats cannot see in total darkness, as some people think. However, cats have an adaptation that affords them excellent night vision. At the back of the eyes is a reflecting layer that sends light through to the sensitive cells leading to the brain. The cells increase the effect of even the smallest amount of light. This layer also makes cats' eyes shine. A cat has a field of vision of 280 degrees.

The teeth are sharp canines. They are used for stabbing and slicing. They are not the flat teeth that vegetarians use for grinding. The claws are very sharp. They are real weapons.

Usually the coat of fur is orange with black stripes. Strange as it may seem, this coloration provides very good camouflage.

Camouflage allows an animal to blend in with its surroundings. In the case of the tiger, the stripes match the tall grasses where it lives. Experienced hunters will tell you that it is almost impossible to spot a tiger in these surroundings. This camouflage is especially effective at dawn and in the evening.

Tigers use camouflage both to protect themselves from hunters and to shield themselves when they are stalking their prey. A tiger may wait quietly in the bushes for an animal to come to a watering hole. Or, it may sneak up on an unsuspecting animal. Either way, camouflage helps it.

Tigers are excellent hunters. They are swift and deadly. They will sneak up on the prey, chase it if necessary, spring on it and bring it to the ground. Tigers are fearless in their attack. They will even go after elephants. They often rest during the day and hunt at night.

There is reason to believe that tigers are not comfortable in very warm climates. They are believed to have originated in northern Asia and migrated southwards. They tend to be active at night. Most of their days are spent "cooling off" in water or sleeping.

Family Life:

The largest tigers are the Siberian and Manchurian tigers. They measure between 11 and 13 feet in length and weigh about 650 pounds. The tiger pictured in this book is the Indian or Bengal tiger. It measures about 9 feet and weighs between 300 and 550 pounds. Smaller tigers live in Malaya and Indonesia.

A baby tiger is called a cub. The period of gestation for tigers is 110 days. Gestation is the time that the baby grows inside its mother's body before it is born. A mother tiger has between two and six cubs at a time. Cubs weigh 2 or 3 pounds at birth. After birth they are blind and helpless. Like most small cats, they are cute, fuzzy balls of curiosity. They have the same marking at birth that they will have all their lives. They do not change color or markings as some animals do when they mature. After several weeks, they begin to play at fighting with each other. These mock fights prepare them for the real thing later on.

Unlike lions, tigers lead a rather solitary life. The male seems to take little interest in his young. The care of the cubs is left to the female. When they are 6 or 8 weeks old she will begin taking them on hunting trips. By the end of a year she will have taught them all they need to know to hunt. When they are 3 or 4 years of age they will leave their mother and go out on their own. They will start raising their own families.

Conservation:

Because the tiger is such a fearless and adept hunter, it is thought to be a valuable sport animal. Tiger hunting has always been a popular pastime for Indian princes. Pitting their courage against the tiger was considered manly. A hunt would involve dozens of elephants and beaters. Beaters are men who travel on foot at the head of a hunting party. They locate the tiger and direct the hunter to it.

In addition to this, the fur of the tiger is highly prized. It is used to make expensive coats.

For sport and fur, hunters have driven the tiger to near extinction. Of the many tigers that once roamed Asia, only about 5,000 of the species still exist. Of the gigantic Manchurian species, only about 200-300 remain. The Javan is the rarest tiger of all. Only about 12 survive.

Many national parks have been established for the preservation of these beautiful animals. Since they breed well in captivity, there is much hope. Two important reserves for tigers are the King George V National Park and the Corbett National Park in northern India.